REFLECTIONS
OF *Love*

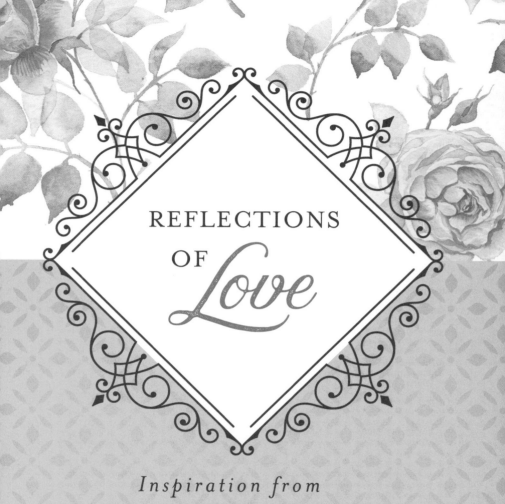

REFLECTIONS

OF

Love

Inspiration from
HELEN STEINER RICE

BARBOUR BOOKS
An Imprint of Barbour Publishing, Inc.

A HELEN STEINER RICE® Product

Published by Barbour Books, an imprint of Barbour Publishing, Inc., 1810 Barbour Drive, Uhrichsville, Ohio 44683, www.barbourbooks.com

Our mission is to inspire the world with the life-changing message of the Bible.

Member of the
Evangelical Christian
Publishers Association

Printed in China.

Contents

God's
Love

*"Though the mountains be shaken and the hills be
removed, yet my unfailing love for you will not be
shaken nor my covenant of peace be removed,"
says the LORD, who has compassion on you.*

ISAIAH 54:10

God loves you, dear friend—constantly, completely, irrevocably. He loves you in spite of your past, in light of your future, and without regard for your social or economic status. God's love is free to all who choose to reach out and take it. Have you opened your heart to the Lover of your soul? Have you felt the glory of being immersed in His love? We do not know why He chooses to love us—only that He does. Praise His name!

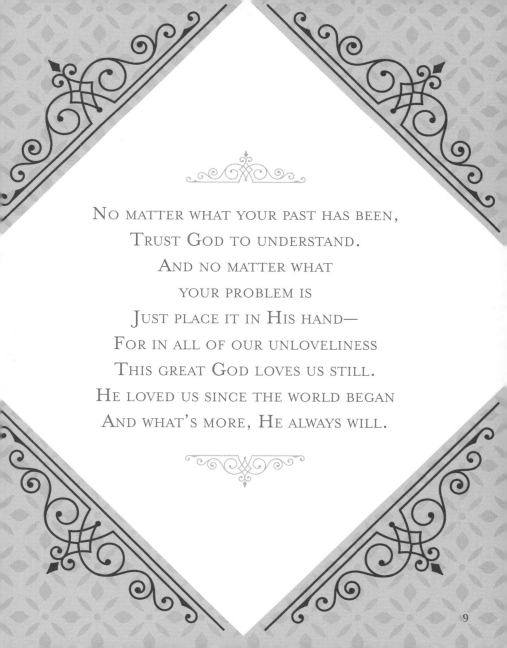

No matter what your past has been,
Trust God to understand.
And no matter what
your problem is
Just place it in His hand—
For in all of our unloveliness
This great God loves us still.
He loved us since the world began
And what's more, He always will.

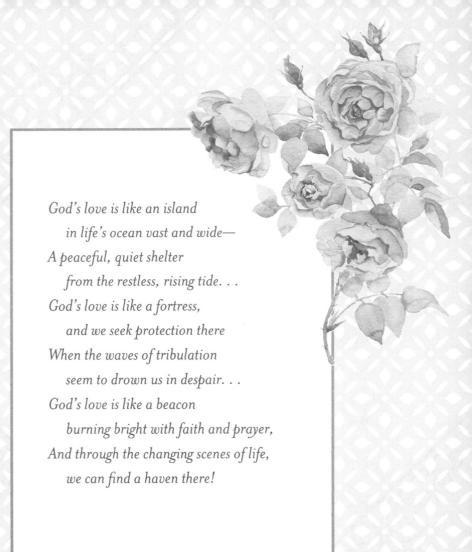

God's love is like an island
    in life's ocean vast and wide—
A peaceful, quiet shelter
    from the restless, rising tide. . .
God's love is like a fortress,
    and we seek protection there
When the waves of tribulation
    seem to drown us in despair. . .
God's love is like a beacon
    burning bright with faith and prayer,
And through the changing scenes of life,
    we can find a haven there!

What more can we ask of our Father
Than to know we are never alone,
That His mercy and love are unfailing,
And He makes all our problems His own.

We are all God's children
and He loves us, every one.
He freely and completely forgives
all that we have done,
Asking only if we're ready
to follow where He leads,
Content that in His wisdom
He will answer all our needs.

*If we confess our sins,
he is faithful and just and will
forgive us our sins and purify us
from all unrighteousness.*

1 JOHN 1:9

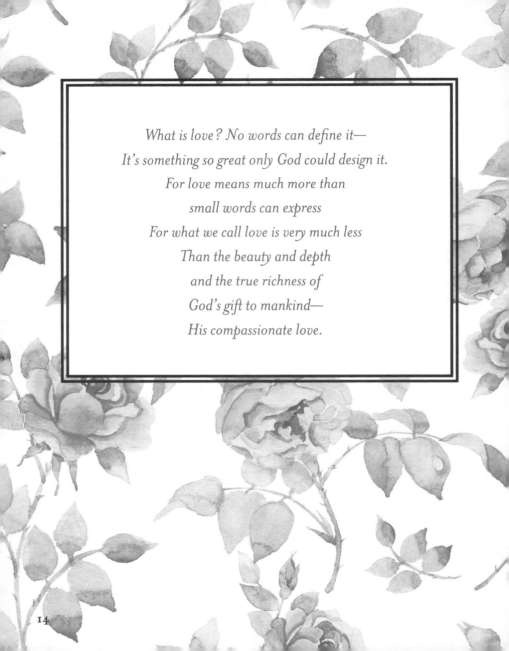

What is love? No words can define it—
It's something so great only God could design it.
For love means much more than
small words can express
For what we call love is very much less
Than the beauty and depth
and the true richness of
God's gift to mankind—
His compassionate love.

Somebody loves you
more than you know,
Somebody goes with you
wherever you go,
Somebody really and truly cares
And lovingly listens
to all of your prayers.
And if you walk in His footsteps
and have faith to believe,
There's nothing you ask for
that you will not receive.

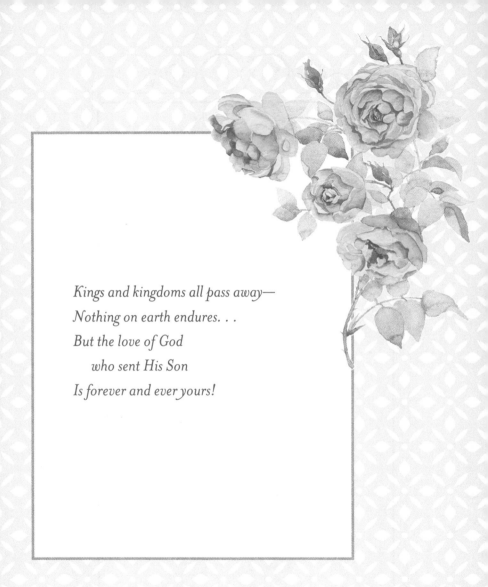

Kings and kingdoms all pass away—
Nothing on earth endures. . .
But the love of God
*   who sent His Son*
Is forever and ever yours!

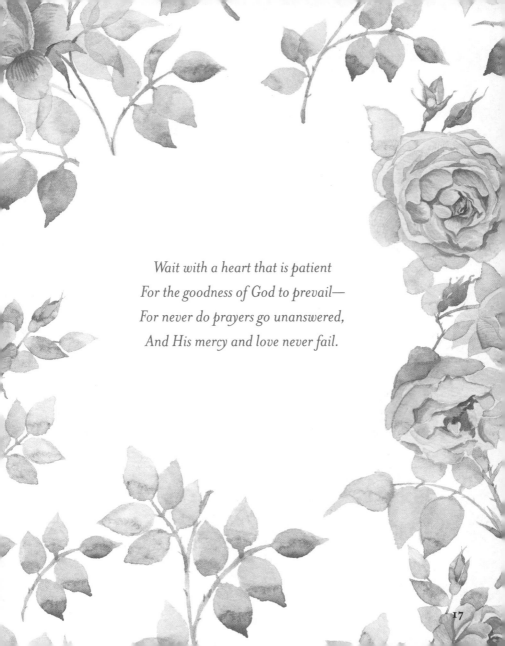

Wait with a heart that is patient
For the goodness of God to prevail—
For never do prayers go unanswered,
And His mercy and love never fail.

God's love is like a sanctuary
where our souls can find sweet rest
From the struggle and the tension
of life's fast and futile quest.

"Come to me, all you
who are weary and burdened,
and I will give you rest."

MATTHEW 11:28

The sky and the stars,
the waves and the sea,
The dew on the grass,
the leaves on the tree
Are constant reminders
of God and His nearness,
Proclaiming His presence
with crystal-like clearness.
So how could I think God
was far, far away
When I feel Him beside me
every hour of the day?
And I've plenty of reasons
to know God's my friend
And this is one friendship
that time cannot end!

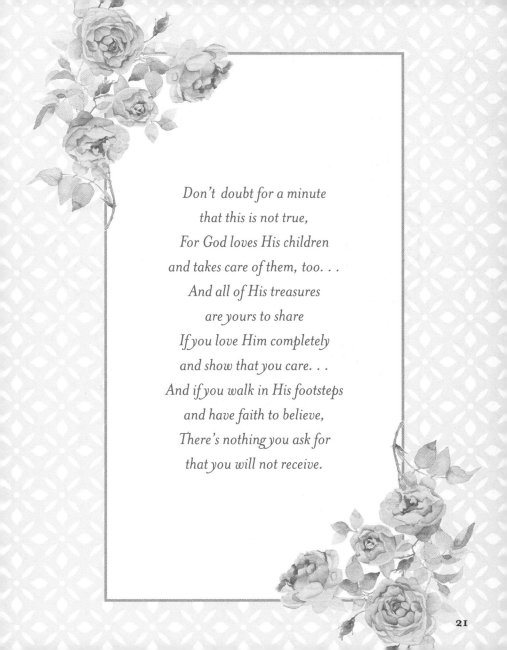

Don't doubt for a minute
that this is not true,
For God loves His children
and takes care of them, too. . .
And all of His treasures
are yours to share
If you love Him completely
and show that you care. . .
And if you walk in His footsteps
and have faith to believe,
There's nothing you ask for
that you will not receive.

Friendship

Two people are better off than one,
for they can help each other succeed.
If one person falls,
the other can reach out and help.

ECCLESIASTES 4:9—10 NLT

The world we live in can be harsh and unwelcoming, intolerant of our mistakes. God knew we would need friends to encourage us along the way. He knew we would need others to laugh with, sing with, dream with. He knew we would need comfort and support and loving-kindness. Cherish your friends; hold them close. They are very special people, for they do God's work in your life.

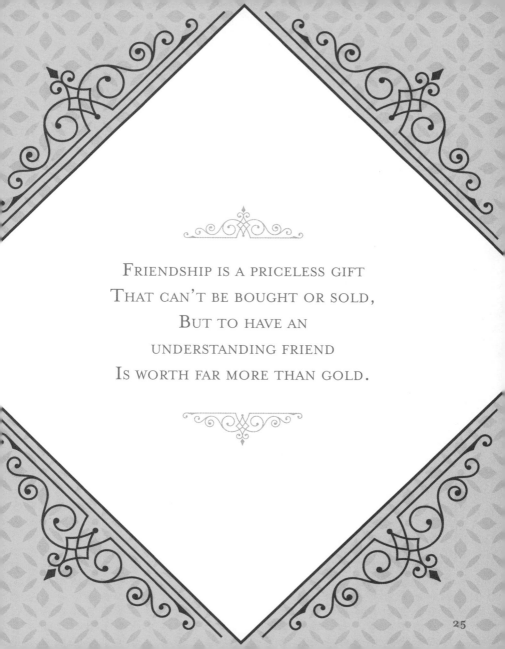

FRIENDSHIP IS A PRICELESS GIFT
THAT CAN'T BE BOUGHT OR SOLD,
BUT TO HAVE AN
UNDERSTANDING FRIEND
IS WORTH FAR MORE THAN GOLD.

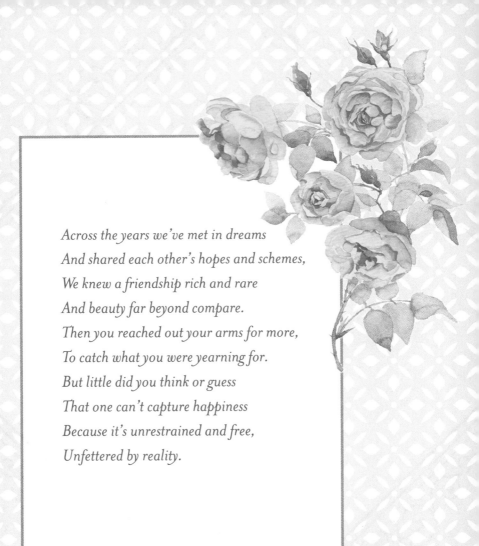

Across the years we've met in dreams
And shared each other's hopes and schemes,
We knew a friendship rich and rare
And beauty far beyond compare.
Then you reached out your arms for more,
To catch what you were yearning for.
But little did you think or guess
That one can't capture happiness
Because it's unrestrained and free,
Unfettered by reality.

We lock up our hearts and fail to heed
The outstretched hand, reaching to find
A kindred spirit whose heart and mind
Are lonely and longing to somehow share
Our joys and sorrows and to make us aware
That life's completeness and richness depends
On the things we share with our loved ones and friends.

Thank you for your friendship
And your understanding of
The folks who truly love you
And the folks you truly love.

"Love one another. As I have loved you, so you must love one another. By this all men will know that you are my disciples, if you love one another."

JOHN 13:34–35

Friends and prayers are priceless treasures
Beyond all monetary measures,
And so I say a special prayer
That God will keep you in His care.

For the friends that we make
are life's gift of love,
And I think friends are sent
right from heaven above.
And thinking of you
somehow makes me feel
That God is love and He's very real.

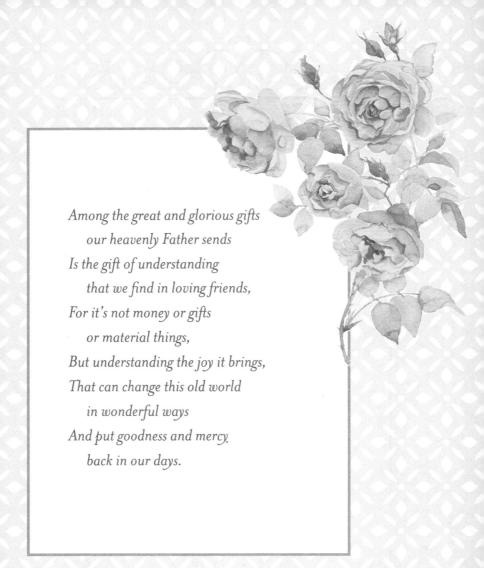

Among the great and glorious gifts
    our heavenly Father sends
Is the gift of understanding
    that we find in loving friends,
For it's not money or gifts
    or material things,
But understanding the joy it brings,
That can change this old world
    in wonderful ways
And put goodness and mercy
    back in our days.

Friendship, like flowers,
blooms ever more fair
When carefully tended by
dear friends who care;
And life's lovely garden
would be sweeter by far
If all who passed through it
were as nice as you are.

If people like me didn't know
people like you,
Life would lose its meaning
and its richness, too.

Every day's a good day
to lose yourself in others
And any time a good time
to see mankind as brothers,
And this can only happen
when you realize it's true
That everyone needs someone
and that someone is you.

Gold is cold and lifeless,
it cannot see nor hear,
And in your times of trouble,
it is powerless to cheer.
It has no ears to listen,
no heart to understand.
It cannot bring you comfort
or reach out a helping hand.
So when you ask God for a gift,
be thankful that He sends,
Not diamonds, pearls, or riches,
but the love of a real, true friend.

Dear children, let us not love with words or tongue but with actions and in truth.

1 JOHN 3:18

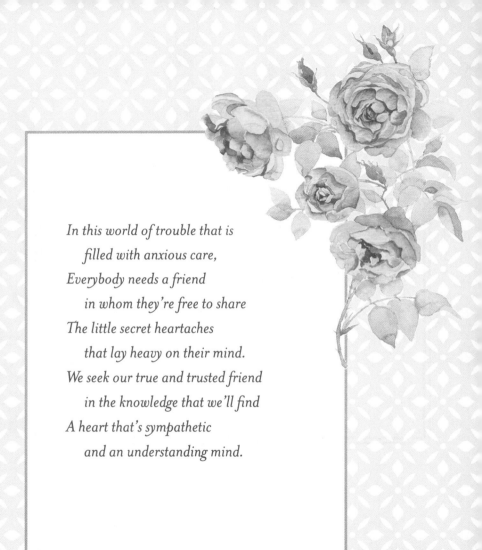

In this world of trouble that is
    filled with anxious care,
Everybody needs a friend
    in whom they're free to share
The little secret heartaches
    that lay heavy on their mind.
We seek our true and trusted friend
    in the knowledge that we'll find
A heart that's sympathetic
    and an understanding mind.

Like roses in a garden,
kindness fills the air
With a certain bit of sweetness
as it touches everywhere.
For kindness is a circle that
never, never ends
But just keeps ever-widening
in the circle of our friends.
For the more you give, the more you
get is proven every day,
And so to get the most from life
you must give yourself away.

You're like a ray of sunshine
Or a star up in the sky,
You add a special brightness
Whenever you pass by.
For in this raucous, restless world
We're small, but God is great,
And in His love, dear friend,
Our hearts communicate!

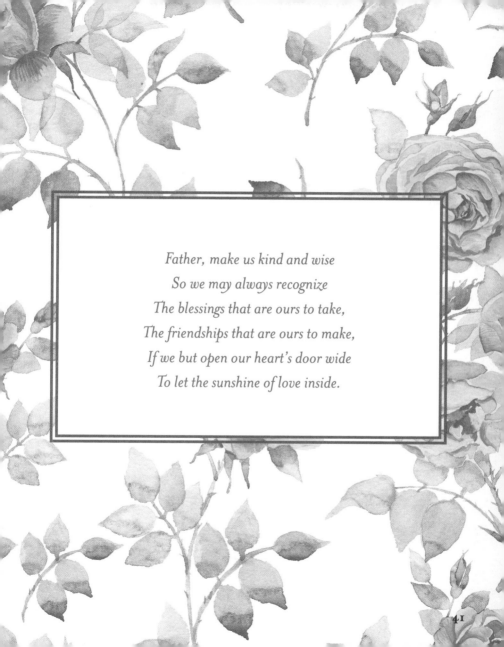

Father, make us kind and wise
So we may always recognize
The blessings that are ours to take,
The friendships that are ours to make,
If we but open our heart's door wide
To let the sunshine of love inside.

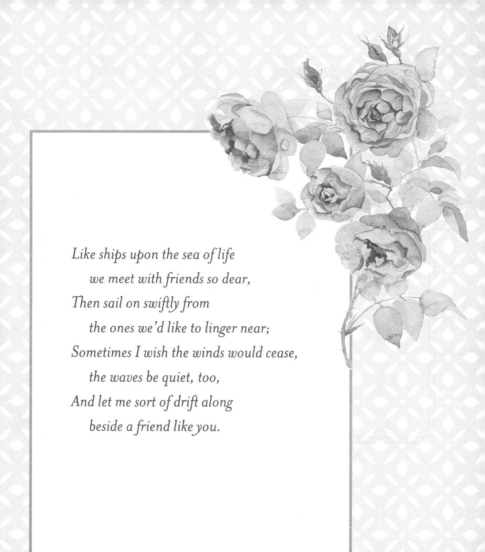

Like ships upon the sea of life
*   we meet with friends so dear,*
Then sail on swiftly from
*   the ones we'd like to linger near;*
Sometimes I wish the winds would cease,
*   the waves be quiet, too,*
And let me sort of drift along
*   beside a friend like you.*

Nothing on earth can make
life more worthwhile
Than a true, loyal friend
and the warmth of a smile,
For just like a sunbeam makes
the cloudy days brighter,
The smile of a friend makes
a heavy heart lighter.

Family

Love must be sincere. Hate what is evil; cling to what is good.
Be devoted to one another in brotherly love.
Honor one another above yourselves.

ROMANS 12:9–10

What is deeper, more constant than a mother's love and a father's love? It is the truest affection we can know. That's how God loves each of us. To prove it, He has placed us in families, where such love can be expressed in human terms— hugs, kisses, verbal assurances, and encouragement. Family is God's gift to us. Thank Him for each member of your biological family, your family of friends, and your spiritual family made up of fellow believers.

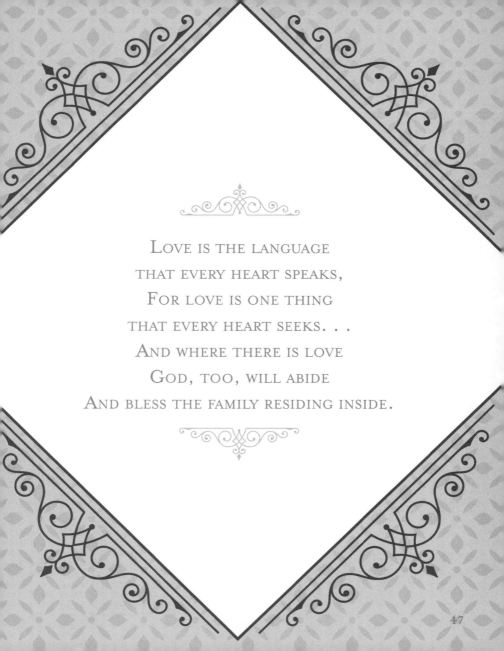

LOVE IS THE LANGUAGE
THAT EVERY HEART SPEAKS,
FOR LOVE IS ONE THING
THAT EVERY HEART SEEKS. . .
AND WHERE THERE IS LOVE
GOD, TOO, WILL ABIDE
AND BLESS THE FAMILY RESIDING INSIDE.

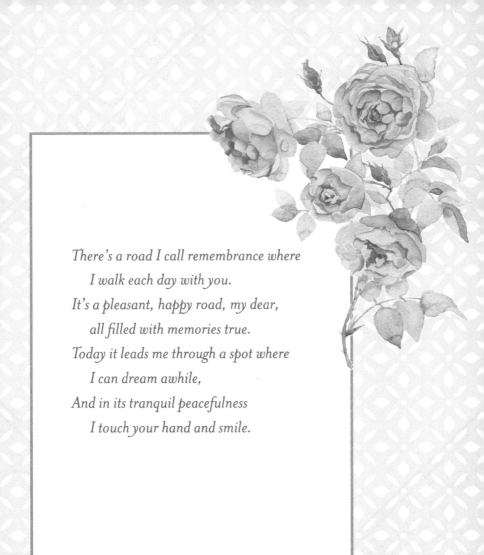

There's a road I call remembrance where
    I walk each day with you.
It's a pleasant, happy road, my dear,
    all filled with memories true.
Today it leads me through a spot where
    I can dream awhile,
And in its tranquil peacefulness
    I touch your hand and smile.

It takes a mother's kindness
to forgive us when we err,
To sympathize in trouble
and bow her head in prayer.
It takes a mother's wisdom
to recognize our needs
And to give us reassurance
by her loving words and deeds.

Tender little memories
of some word or deed
Give us strength and courage
when we are in need.
Blessed little memories
help to bear the cross
And soften all the bitterness
of failure and of loss.
Precious little memories
of little things we've done
Make the very darkest day
a bright and happy one.

The Lord reigns, let the earth be glad;
let the distant shores rejoice.

PSALM 97:1

Memories to treasure
are made every day—
Made of family gatherings
and children as they play.

A mother's love is something
that no one can explain—
It is made of deep devotion
and sacrifice and pain.
It believes beyond believing
when the world around condemns,
And it glows with all the beauty
of the rarest, brightest gems.
A many–splendored miracle
we cannot understand
And another wondrous evidence
of God's tender, guiding hand.

Across the years
we've met in dreams
And shared each other's
hopes and schemes,
We knew a friendship
rich and rare
And beauty far
beyond compare.

A mother's love is like an island
In life's ocean vast and wide—
A peaceful, quiet shelter
From the restless, rising tide.
A mother's love is like a beacon
Burning bright with faith and prayer,
And through the changing scenes of life,
We can find a haven there.
For a mother's love is fashioned
After God's enduring love—
It is endless and unfailing
Like the love of Him above.

In seeking peace for all people
There is only one place to begin
And that is in each home and heart—
For the fortress of peace is within.

In my eyes there lies no vision
but the sight of your dear face.
In my heart there is no feeling
but the warmth of your embrace.
In my mind there are no thoughts
but the thoughts of you, my dear.
In my soul no other longing
but just to have you near.
All my dreams were built around you,
and I've come to know it's true,
In my life there is no living
that is not a part of you.

Where the home is filled with love
You'll always find God spoken of,
And when a family prays together
That family also stays together.

*Ascribe to the L*ORD *the glory
due his name; worship the L*ORD
in the splendor of his holiness.

PSALM 29:2

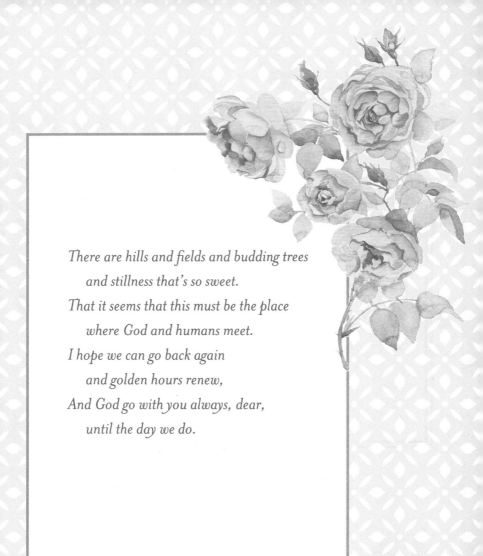

There are hills and fields and budding trees
and stillness that's so sweet.
That it seems that this must be the place
where God and humans meet.
I hope we can go back again
and golden hours renew,
And God go with you always, dear,
until the day we do.

It is sharing and caring,
Giving and forgiving,
Loving and being loved,
Walking hand in hand,
Talking heart to heart,
Seeing through each other's eyes,
Laughing together,
Weeping together,
Praying together,
And always trusting and believing
And thanking God for each other. . .
For love that is shared
is a beautiful thing—
It enriches the soul and
makes the heart sing.

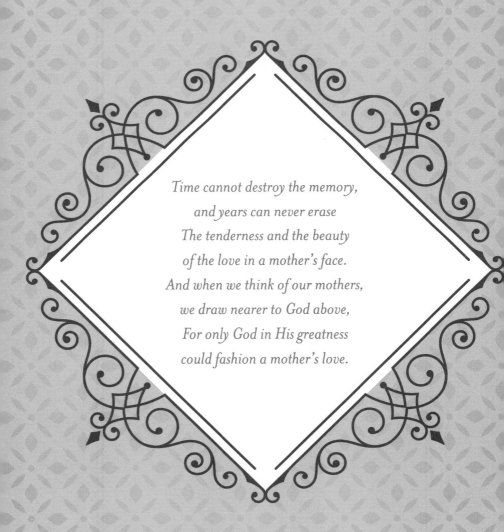

Time cannot destroy the memory,
and years can never erase
The tenderness and the beauty
of the love in a mother's face.
And when we think of our mothers,
we draw nearer to God above,
For only God in His greatness
could fashion a mother's love.

A baby is a gift of life born of
the wonder of love—
A little bit of eternity sent
from the Father above,
Giving a new dimension to the
love between husband and wife
And putting an added new meaning
to the wonder and mystery of life.

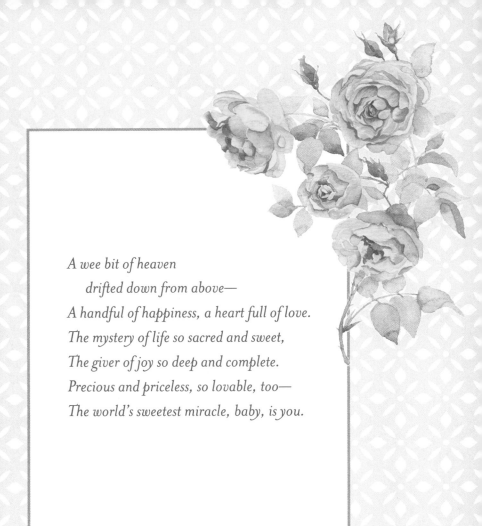

A wee bit of heaven
    drifted down from above—
A handful of happiness, a heart full of love.
The mystery of life so sacred and sweet,
The giver of joy so deep and complete.
Precious and priceless, so lovable, too—
The world's sweetest miracle, baby, is you.

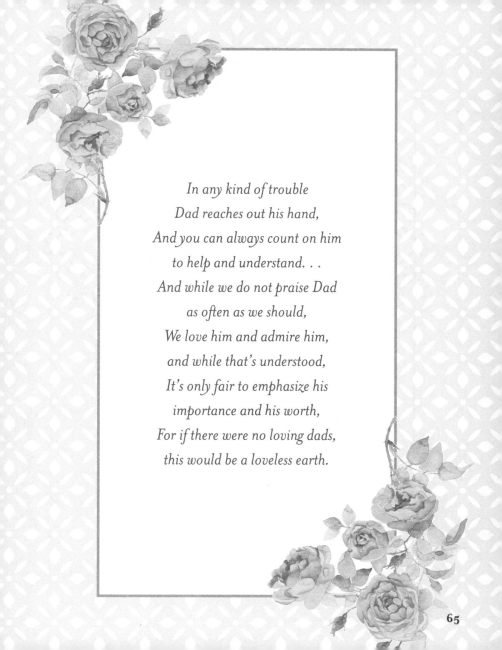

In any kind of trouble
Dad reaches out his hand,
And you can always count on him
to help and understand. . .
And while we do not praise Dad
as often as we should,
We love him and admire him,
and while that's understood,
It's only fair to emphasize his
importance and his worth,
For if there were no loving dads,
this would be a loveless earth.

Love's Power

We are more than conquerors through him who loved us. For I am convinced that neither death nor life, neither angels nor demons, neither the present nor the future, nor any powers, neither height nor depth, nor anything else in all creation, will be able to separate us from the love of God that is in Christ Jesus our Lord.

ROMANS 8:37–39

God's love is powerful enough to save us from ourselves and transform our lives. It can reach to any height or depth. It has no limitations. When we love others, we are like Him—powerful! We can encourage the weary soul, comfort the bereaved, revive the downhearted. We can change lives and inspire eternal results. God's power is in His love, His power to heal and restore. Receive His love, and pass it on to others.

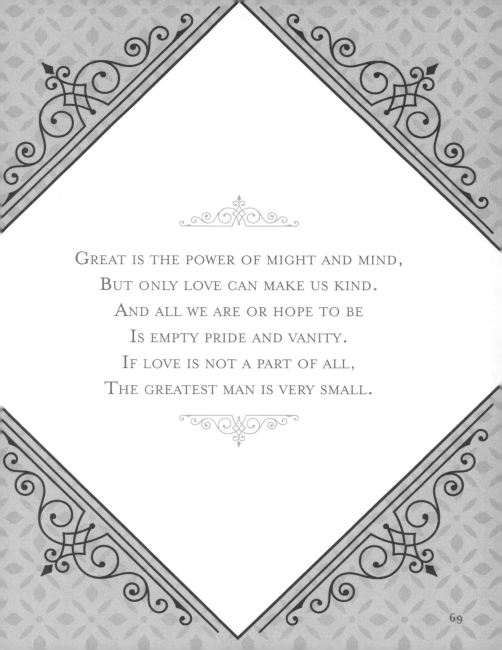

GREAT IS THE POWER OF MIGHT AND MIND,
BUT ONLY LOVE CAN MAKE US KIND.
AND ALL WE ARE OR HOPE TO BE
IS EMPTY PRIDE AND VANITY.
IF LOVE IS NOT A PART OF ALL,
THE GREATEST MAN IS VERY SMALL.

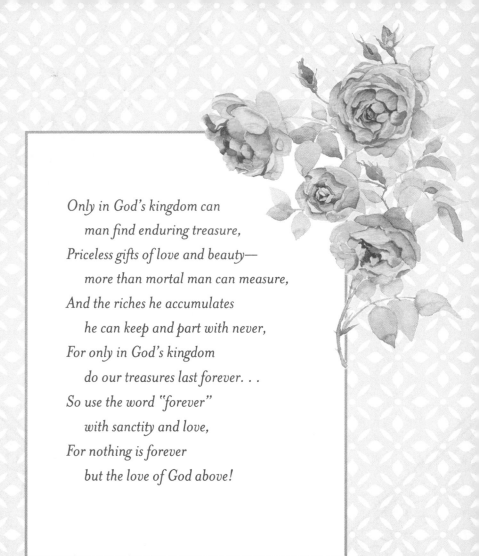

Only in God's kingdom can
 man find enduring treasure,
Priceless gifts of love and beauty—
 more than mortal man can measure,
And the riches he accumulates
 he can keep and part with never,
For only in God's kingdom
 do our treasures last forever. . .
So use the word "forever"
 with sanctity and love,
For nothing is forever
 but the love of God above!

To be in God's keeping
is surely a blessing,
For though life is often
dark and distressing,
No day is too dark
and no burden too great
That God in His love
cannot penetrate.

Love can transform
the most commonplace
Into beauty and kindness
and goodness and grace.

But the fruit of the Spirit is love, joy, peace, patience, kindness, goodness, faithfulness, gentleness and self-control. Against such things there is no law.

GALATIANS 5:22–23

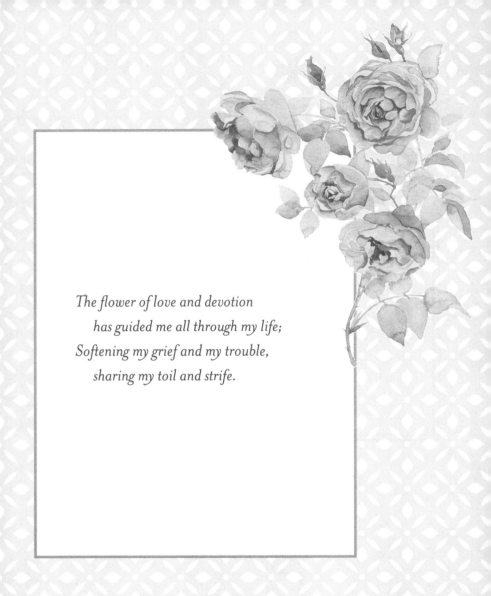

The flower of love and devotion
　　has guided me all through my life;
Softening my grief and my trouble,
　　sharing my toil and strife.

Love is beyond what man can define
For love is immortal
and God's gift is divine.

Love's too great to understand,
But just to clasp a loved one's hand
Can change the darkness into light
And make the heart take wingless flight.

With love in our hearts,
let us try this year
To lift the clouds of hate and fear,
For love works in ways
that are wondrous and strange,
And there is nothing in life
that love cannot change.

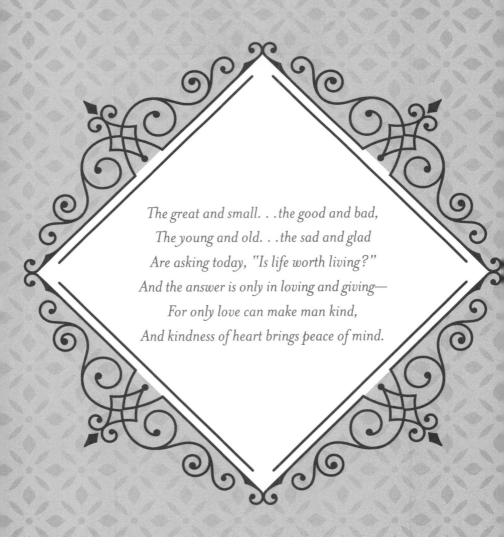

The great and small. . .the good and bad,
The young and old. . .the sad and glad
Are asking today, "Is life worth living?"
And the answer is only in loving and giving—
For only love can make man kind,
And kindness of heart brings peace of mind.

Man is powerless alone
to clean up the world outside
Until his own polluted soul
is clean and free inside. . .
For the amazing power of love
is beyond all comprehension
And it alone can heal this world
of its hatred and dissension.

Love is enduring and
patient and kind,
It judges all things
with the heart, not the mind.
And love can transform
the most commonplace
Into beauty and splendor
and sweetness and grace.

"Love one another.
As I have loved you,
so you must love one another."

JOHN 13:34

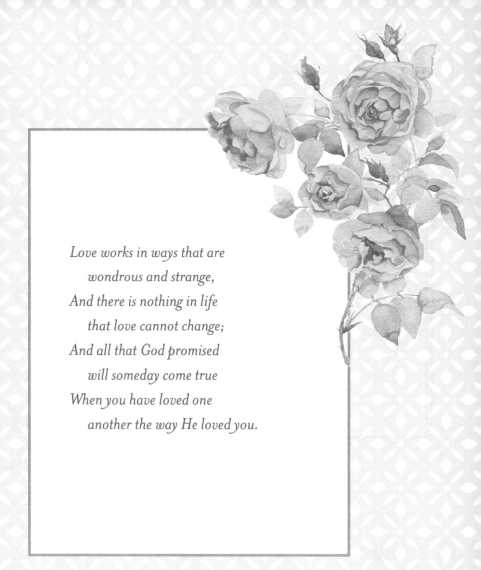

Love works in ways that are
wondrous and strange,
And there is nothing in life
that love cannot change;
And all that God promised
will someday come true
When you have loved one
another the way He loved you.

Love is unselfish,
understanding, and kind,
For it sees with its heart
and not with its mind.
Love is the answer that everyone seeks—
Love is the language
that every heart speaks—
Love can't be bought,
it is priceless and free,
Love, like pure magic, is a sweet mystery.

Love's
Comfort

There is no fear in love.
But perfect love drives out fear.

1 JOHN 4:18

You may be at a low point in your life, dear friend. You may have suffered tragedy or disappointment or discouragement. You are not alone. God is at your side. If you will let Him, He is eager to help carry your burden. He longs to comfort you and remind you of the blessings in your life. Open your heart to Him. Invite Him to help you with your trouble. He will not disappoint you.

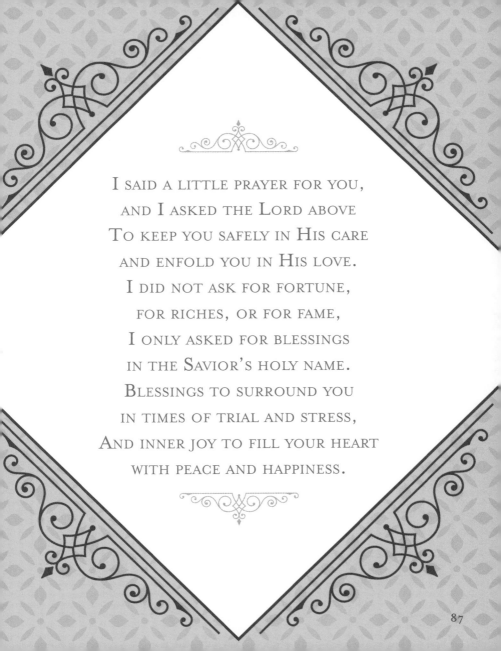

I SAID A LITTLE PRAYER FOR YOU,
AND I ASKED THE LORD ABOVE
TO KEEP YOU SAFELY IN HIS CARE
AND ENFOLD YOU IN HIS LOVE.
I DID NOT ASK FOR FORTUNE,
FOR RICHES, OR FOR FAME,
I ONLY ASKED FOR BLESSINGS
IN THE SAVIOR'S HOLY NAME.
BLESSINGS TO SURROUND YOU
IN TIMES OF TRIAL AND STRESS,
AND INNER JOY TO FILL YOUR HEART
WITH PEACE AND HAPPINESS.

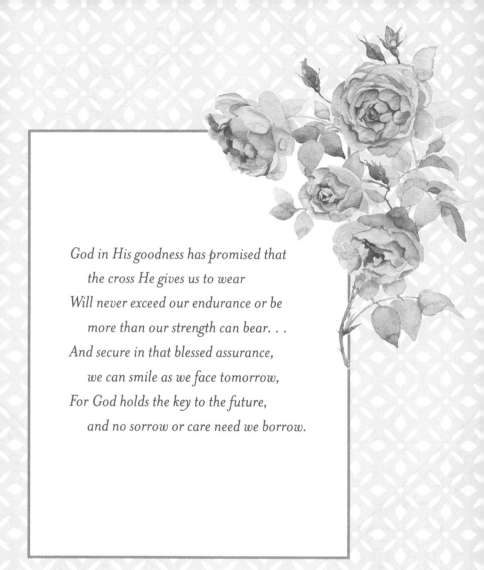

God in His goodness has promised that
the cross He gives us to wear
Will never exceed our endurance or be
more than our strength can bear. . .
And secure in that blessed assurance,
we can smile as we face tomorrow,
For God holds the key to the future,
and no sorrow or care need we borrow.

The earth is the Lord's
and the fullness thereof,
It speaks of His greatness
and it sings of His love.
It whispers of mysteries
we cannot comprehend,
Of a beautiful land
where life has no end.

Thank You, God, for the beauty
around me everywhere:
The gentle rain and glistening dew,
the sunshine and the air,
The joyous gift of feeling the
soul's soft, whispering voice,
That speaks to me from deep within
and makes my heart rejoice.

Always giving thanks to God the Father for everything, in the name of our Lord Jesus Christ.

EPHESIANS 5:20

I am the Way, so just follow Me
Though the way be rough
and you cannot see.
I am the Truth, which all men seek,
So heed not false prophets
or the words that they speak.
I am the Life and I hold the key
That opens the door to eternity.
And in this dark world,
I am the Light
To a Promised Land
where there is no night.

His love knows no exceptions
so never feel excluded;
No matter who or what you are,
your name has been included—
And no matter what your past has been,
trust God to understand,
And no matter what your problem is
just place it in His hand.

I know He stilled the tempest
and calmed the angry sea,
And I humbly ask if in His love
He'll do the same for me.

God, be my resting place
and my protection
In hours of trouble, defeat,
and dejection.
May I never give way
to self-pity and sorrow,
May I always be sure
of a better tomorrow.
May I stand undaunted,
come what may,
Secure in the knowledge
I have only to pray
And ask my Creator
and Father above
To keep me serene
in His grace and His love.

The love of God surrounds us
Like the air we breathe around us—
As near as a heartbeat,
as close as a prayer,
And whenever we need Him,
He'll always be there.

"*And surely I am with you always,
to the very end of the age.*"

MATTHEW 28:20

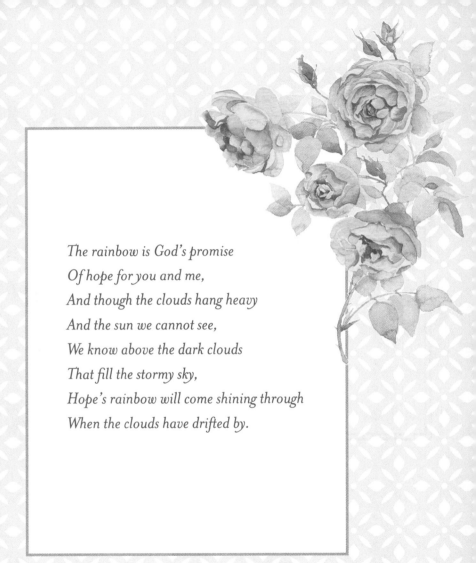

The rainbow is God's promise
Of hope for you and me,
And though the clouds hang heavy
And the sun we cannot see,
We know above the dark clouds
That fill the stormy sky,
Hope's rainbow will come shining through
When the clouds have drifted by.

Someone cares and always will,
The world forgets
but God loves you still,
You cannot go beyond His love
No matter what you're guilty of—
Someone cares and loves you still
And God is the someone
who always will.

Love's
Pricelessness

How priceless is your unfailing love!
Both high and low among men find
refuge in the shadow of your wings.

PSALM 36:7

How can the price of God's love be measured? He loved us
enough to create us. He loved us enough to give us a free will.
He loved us enough to pay the highest imaginable price to buy
us back when we chose poorly and gave ourselves to another.
Even now, He loves us more than we can know. He lovingly
hears our prayers and guides our steps. God's love is not free,
but it will cost you nothing, dear friend. Reach out to Him,
and you will receive.

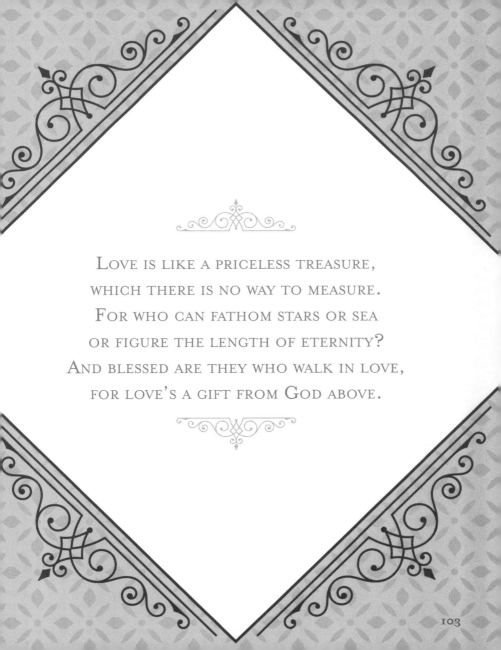

LOVE IS LIKE A PRICELESS TREASURE,
WHICH THERE IS NO WAY TO MEASURE.
FOR WHO CAN FATHOM STARS OR SEA
OR FIGURE THE LENGTH OF ETERNITY?
AND BLESSED ARE THEY WHO WALK IN LOVE,
FOR LOVE'S A GIFT FROM GOD ABOVE.

It can't be bought, it can't be sold.
It can't be measured in silver or gold.
It's a special wish that God above
Will fill your heart
    with peace and love—
The love of God, which is divine,
That is beyond what words can define,
So you may know the comfort of
God's all-fulfilling grace and love.

Love means much more
than small words can express,
For what we call love
is so very much less
Than the beauty and depth
and the true richness of
God's gift to mankind—
His compassionate love.

The priceless gift of life is love.
For with the help of God above,
Love dissolves all hate and fear
And makes our vision bright and clear,
So we can see and rise above
Our pettiness on wings of love.

A man's wisdom gives him patience;
it is to his glory to overlook an offense.

PROVERBS 19:11

Love is a gift to treasure forever
Given by God without price tag or measure. . .
Love is a gift we all can possess,
Love is a key to the soul's happiness.

Love is much more than a tender caress
And more than bright hours of happiness,
For a lasting love is made up of sharing
Both hours that are joyous
and also despairing.
It's made up of patience
and deep understanding
And never of stubborn
or selfish demanding.
It's made up of climbing
the steep hills together
And facing with courage
life's stormiest weather.

Love is unselfish, understanding, and kind,
For it sees with its heart
and not with its mind.

Love can't be bought—
it is priceless and free.
Love, like pure magic,
is a sweet mystery.

Love is the answer
that everyone seeks.
Love is the language
that every heart speaks.

Love covers over all wrongs.

PROVERBS 10:12

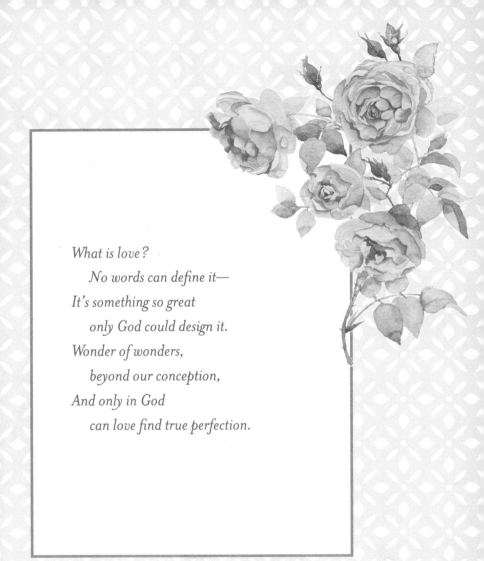

What is love?
      No words can define it—
It's something so great
      only God could design it.
Wonder of wonders,
      beyond our conception,
And only in God
      can love find true perfection.

With our hands we give
gifts that money can buy—
Diamonds that sparkle
like stars in the sky,
Trinkets that glitter
like the sun as it rises,
Beautiful baubles
that come as surprises—
But only our hearts
can feel real love
And share the gift
of our Father above.

Loving
Others

We know what real love is because Jesus gave up his life for us.
So we also ought to give up our lives for our brothers and sisters.

1 JOHN 3:16 NLT

God's love, dear friend, cannot be contained. It fills the willing heart to overflowing and the result is that we love others as He has loved us. Every kindness, every tenderness, every word of encouragement, every smile, every loving act springs from the divine fountain that gushes forth from our souls. Have you received God's love? Then you need only do what comes naturally—allow His love to flow to others.

EVERY DAY'S A GOOD DAY TO
LOSE YOURSELF IN OTHERS
AND ANY TIME A GOOD TIME
TO SEE MANKIND AS BROTHERS,
AND THIS CAN ONLY HAPPEN
WHEN YOU REALIZE IT'S TRUE
THAT EVERYONE NEEDS SOMEONE
AND THAT SOMEONE IS YOU!

Every day is a reason for giving,
And giving is the key to living.
So let us give ourselves away,
Not just today but every day.

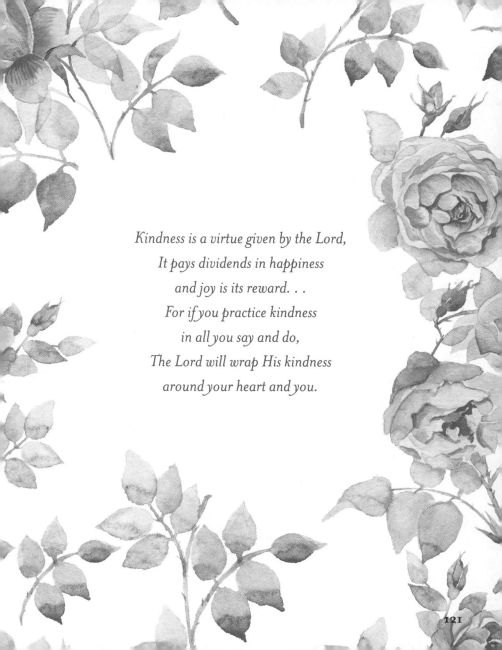

Kindness is a virtue given by the Lord,
It pays dividends in happiness
and joy is its reward. . .
For if you practice kindness
in all you say and do,
The Lord will wrap His kindness
around your heart and you.

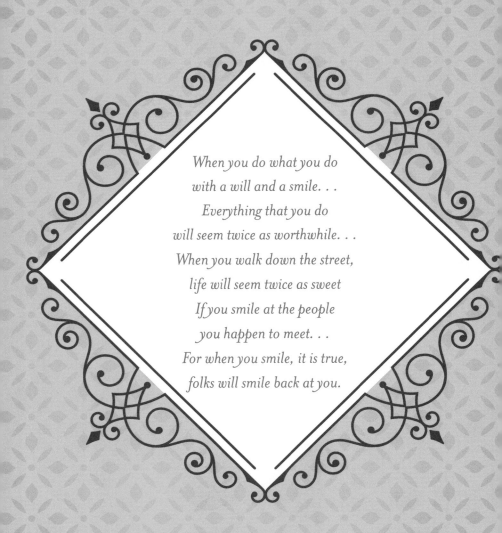

When you do what you do
with a will and a smile. . .
Everything that you do
will seem twice as worthwhile. . .
When you walk down the street,
life will seem twice as sweet
If you smile at the people
you happen to meet. . .
For when you smile, it is true,
folks will smile back at you.

Rejoice in the Lord always.
I will say it again: Rejoice!

PHILIPPIANS 4:4

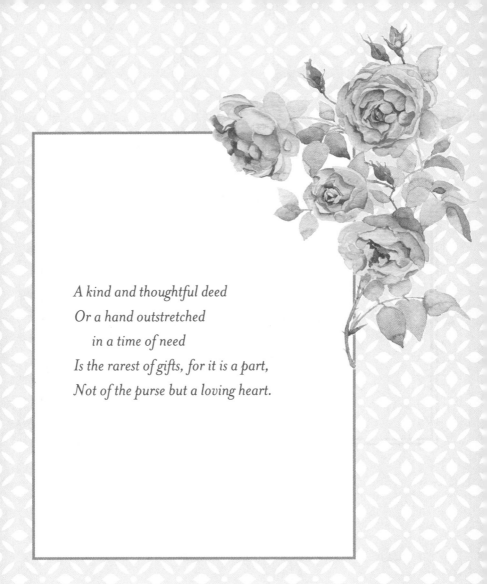

A kind and thoughtful deed
Or a hand outstretched
in a time of need
Is the rarest of gifts, for it is a part,
Not of the purse but a loving heart.

The more you give,
the more you get—
The more you laugh,
the less you fret—
The more you do unselfishly,
The more you live abundantly.

The more of everything you share,
The more you'll always have to spare—
The more you love, the more you'll find
That life is good and friends are kind. . .
For only what we give away,
enriches us from day to day.

No one is a stranger in God's sight,
For God is love and in His light
May we, too, try in our small way
To make new friends from day to day. . .
So pass no stranger with an unseeing eye,
For God may be sending a new friend by.

To love one another
as God loved you
May seem impossible to do,
But if you will try
to have faith and believe
There's no end
to the joy that you will receive.

Therefore, as God's chosen people,
holy and dearly loved, clothe yourselves
with compassion, kindness, humility,
gentleness and patience.

COLOSSIANS 3:12

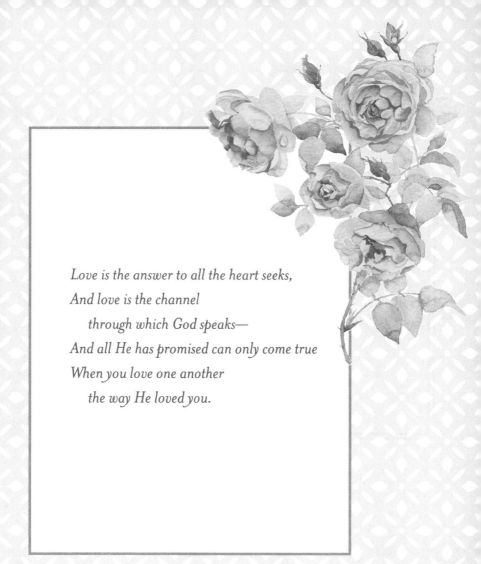

Love is the answer to all the heart seeks,
And love is the channel
*   through which God speaks—*
And all He has promised can only come true
When you love one another
*   the way He loved you.*

Great is our gladness
to serve God through others,
For our Father taught us
we all are sisters and brothers,
And the people we meet
on life's thoroughfares
Are burdened with trouble
and sorrow and cares,
And this is the chance
we are given each day
To witness for God,
to learn and obey.

A cheerful smile, a friendly word,
a sympathetic nod,
All priceless little treasures
from the storehouse of our God—
They are the things that can't be
bought with silver or with gold,
For thoughtfulness and kindness
and love are never sold—
They are the priceless things in life
for which no one can pay,
And the giver finds rich recompense
in giving them away.

Only what we give away
Enriches us from day to day,
For not in getting but in giving
Is found the lasting joy of living,
For no one ever had a part
In sharing treasures of the heart
Who did not feel the impact of
The magic mystery of God's love.
Love alone can make us kind
And give us joy and peace of mind,
So live with joy unselfishly
And you'll be blessed abundantly.

Romance, Commitment & Marriage

Most important of all, continue to show deep love
for each other, for love covers a multitude of sins.

1 PETER 4:8 NLT

Marriage is a sturdy structure, designed to provide love and intimacy and companionship throughout our lives. It is more than romance. It is romance plus commitment—so that we don't lose our bearings when the feelings ebb and flow. Rejoice in the one God has given you, dear friend. Being true to your spouse is being true to God. He will be pleased by your faithfulness and love.

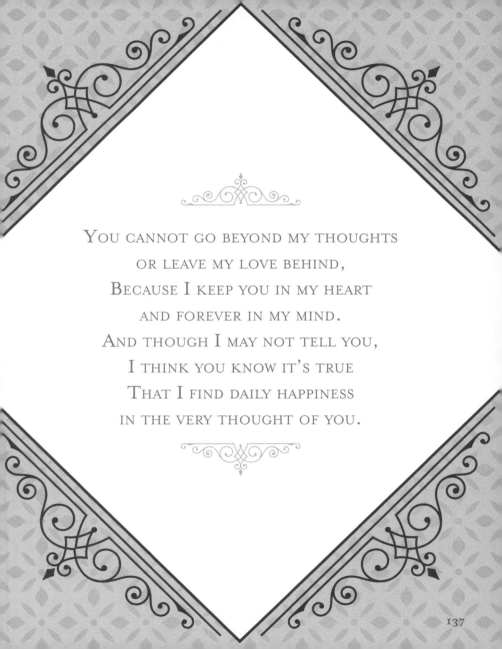

YOU CANNOT GO BEYOND MY THOUGHTS
OR LEAVE MY LOVE BEHIND,
BECAUSE I KEEP YOU IN MY HEART
AND FOREVER IN MY MIND.
AND THOUGH I MAY NOT TELL YOU,
I THINK YOU KNOW IT'S TRUE
THAT I FIND DAILY HAPPINESS
IN THE VERY THOUGHT OF YOU.

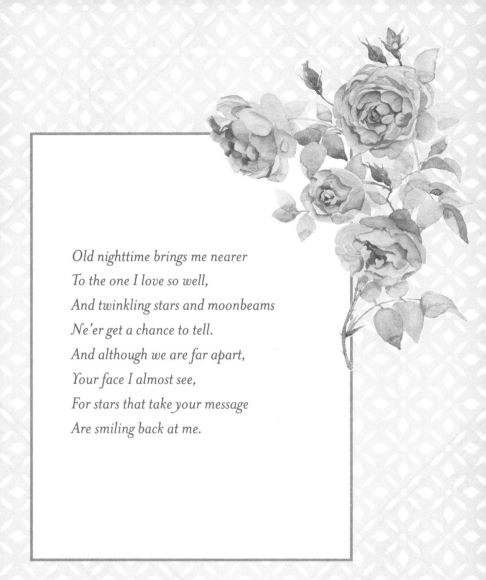

Old nighttime brings me nearer
To the one I love so well,
And twinkling stars and moonbeams
Ne'er get a chance to tell.
And although we are far apart,
Your face I almost see,
For stars that take your message
Are smiling back at me.

There is comfort just in longing
For a smile from your dear face,
And joy in just remembering
Each sweet and fond embrace.
There is happiness in knowing
That my heart will always be
A place where I can hold you
And keep you near to me.

Love is a many-splendored thing,
The greatest joy that life can bring,
And let no one try to disparage
The sacred bond of holy marriage,
For love is not love until God above
Sanctifies the union of two people in love.

Marriage should be honored by all.

HEBREWS 13:4

What is marriage?
It is sharing and caring,
Giving and forgiving,
Loving and being loved,
Walking hand in hand,
Talking heart to heart,
Seeing through each other's eyes,
Laughing together,
Weeping together,
Praying together,
And always trusting and believing
And thanking God for each other...
For love that is shared is a beautiful thing—
It enriches the soul and makes the heart sing.

In my eyes there lies no vision
but the sight of your dear face,
In my heart there is no feeling
but the warmth of your embrace.
In my mind there are no thoughts
but the thoughts of you, my dear,
In my soul no other longing
but just to have you near.
All my dreams are built around you,
and I've come to know it's true,
In my life there is no living
that is not a part of you.

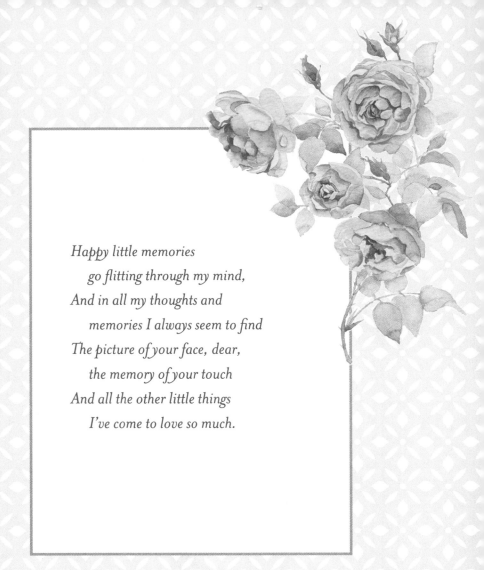

Happy little memories
  go flitting through my mind,
And in all my thoughts and
  memories I always seem to find
The picture of your face, dear,
  the memory of your touch
And all the other little things
  I've come to love so much.

There's a heap of satisfaction
to sit here thinking of you
And to tell you once again, dear,
how very much I love you.

Dear God,
Please help me in my feeble way
To somehow do something each day
To show the one I love the best
My faith in him will stand each test.
And let me show in some small way
The love I have for him each day
And prove beyond all doubt and fear
That his love for me
I hold most dear.
And so I ask of God above—
Just make me worthy of his love.

Submit to one another out
of reverence for Christ.

EPHESIANS 5:21

There are things we cannot measure,
like the depths of waves and sea
And the heights of stars in heaven
and the joy you bring to me.
Like eternity's long endlessness
and the sunset's golden hue,
There is no way to measure
the love I have for you.

You put the love in loveliness
And the sweet in sweetness, too.
I think they took
life's dearest things
And wrapped them up in you.
So keep me in your heart, dear,
And in your every prayer,
For wherever you are, darling,
I like to feel I'm there.

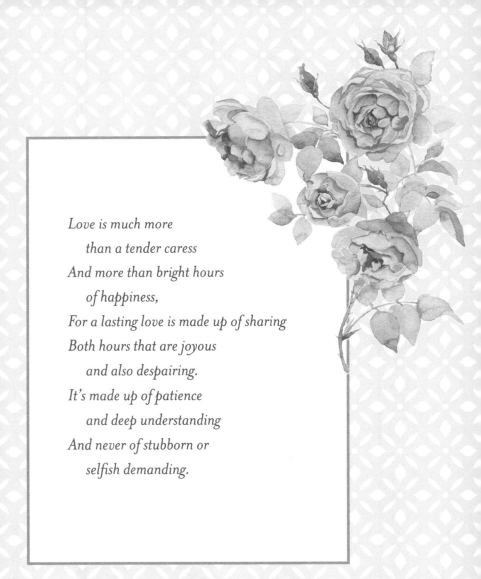

Love is much more
than a tender caress
And more than bright hours
of happiness,
For a lasting love is made up of sharing
Both hours that are joyous
and also despairing.
It's made up of patience
and deep understanding
And never of stubborn or
selfish demanding.

You're lovable; you're wonderful;
You're as sweet as you can be.
There's no one in all the world
Who means so much to me;
I love you more than life itself,
You make my dreams come true,
Forever is not long enough
For me to be near to you.

Healing Love

Confess your sins to each other and pray for each other so that you may be healed. The earnest prayer of a righteous person has great power and produces wonderful results.

JAMES 5:16 NLT

The love of God does many things in our lives—but most of all, it heals us. It transforms our broken lives and squandered possibilities into tapestries of great beauty. It makes all things new. No matter how old you are, how much water has passed under the bridge in your life, how many mistakes you've made, with God you have the chance to begin tomorrow with hope, dear friend. He is the God who heals you.

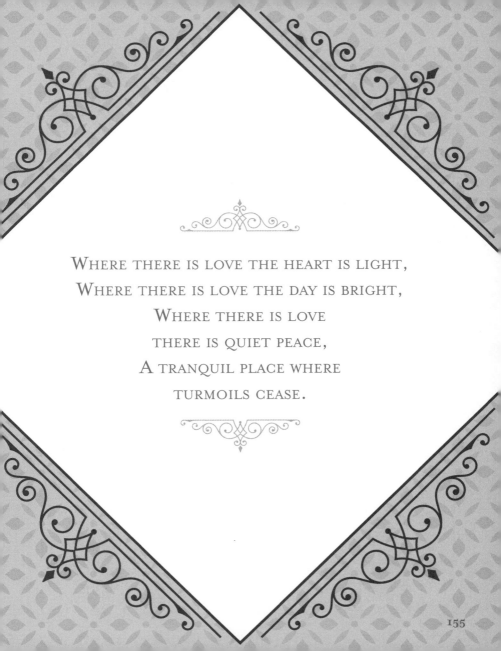

WHERE THERE IS LOVE THE HEART IS LIGHT,
WHERE THERE IS LOVE THE DAY IS BRIGHT,
WHERE THERE IS LOVE
THERE IS QUIET PEACE,
A TRANQUIL PLACE WHERE
TURMOILS CEASE.

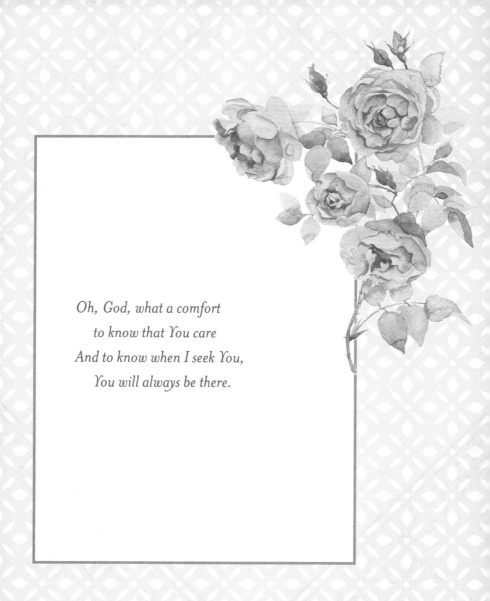

Oh, God, what a comfort
to know that You care
And to know when I seek You,
You will always be there.

May He who lived in Galilee
And healed the many there
Be near to you and heal you, too,
And keep you in His care.

Not money or gifts
or material things,
But understanding and
the joy it brings,
Can change this old world
in wonderful ways
And put goodness and mercy
back in our days.

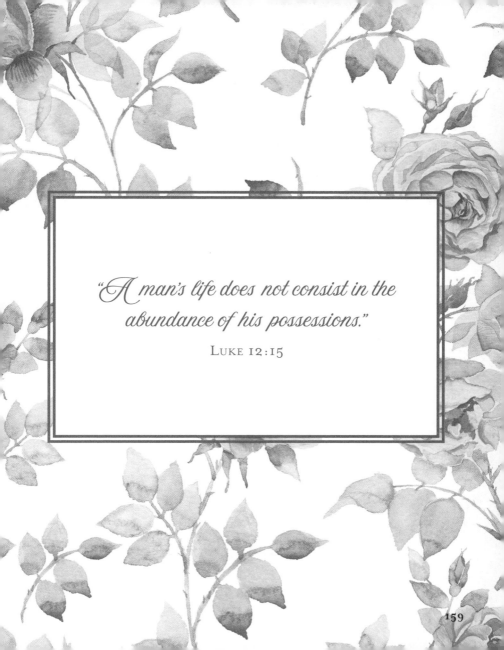

"A man's life does not consist in the
abundance of his possessions."

LUKE 12:15

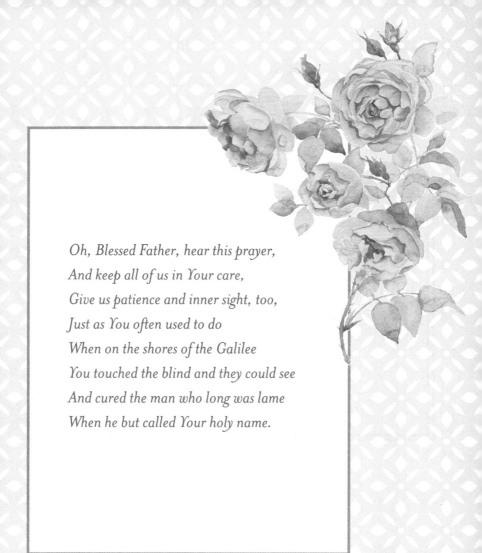

Oh, Blessed Father, hear this prayer,
And keep all of us in Your care,
Give us patience and inner sight, too,
Just as You often used to do
When on the shores of the Galilee
You touched the blind and they could see
And cured the man who long was lame
When he but called Your holy name.

While life's a mystery
we can't understand
The great Giver of life
is holding our hand,
And safe in His care
there is no need for seeing,
For in Him we live and
move and have our being.

All around on every side,
new life and joy appear
To tell us nothing ever dies
and we should have no fear,
For death is just a detour
along life's winding way
That leads God's chosen children
to a bright and glorious day.

Love is the key
that throws open the door
To the heart that was locked
and lonely before.

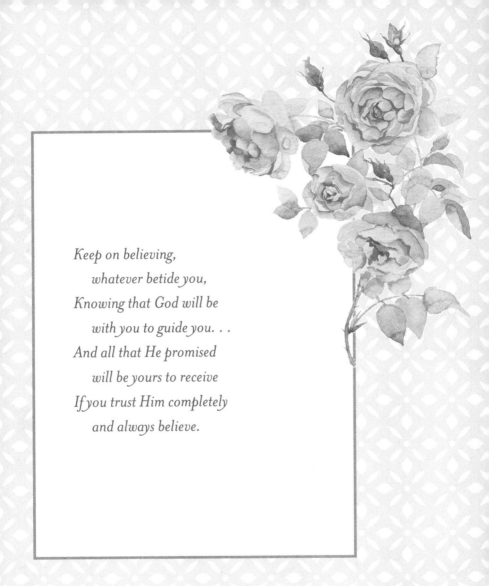

Keep on believing,
whatever betide you,
Knowing that God will be
with you to guide you...
And all that He promised
will be yours to receive
If you trust Him completely
and always believe.

"If you believe, you will receive what-
ever you ask for in prayer."

MATTHEW 21:22

When you're troubled and
worried and sick at heart
And your plans are upset
and your world falls apart,
Remember God's ready
and waiting to share
The burden you find
too heavy to bear.
So with faith, let go and let
God lead the way
Into a brighter and less troubled day.

In sickness or health,
In suffering and pain,
In storm-laden skies,
In sunshine and rain,
God always is there
To lighten your way
And lead you through darkness
To a much brighter day.

The house of prayer is no farther away
Than the quiet spot
where you kneel and pray,
For the heart is a temple
when God is there
As you place yourself in His loving care.

God can remove our uncertain fear
And replace our worry
with healing cheer. . .
So close your eyes and open your heart
And let God come in and freely impart
A brighter outlook
and new courage, too,
As His spiritual sunshine
smiles on you.

Eternal
Love

*Three things will last forever—faith, hope,
and love—and the greatest of these is love.*

1 Corinthians 13:13 NLT

Even the most exquisite forms of human love are fallible. But God's love never fails. It does not change with circumstances or seek revenge when it is rebuffed. God's love is pure—and it's eternal. It provides shelter from the storms of life and more joy than the human heart can contain. It is the basis for which all love exists. Submit your lonely heart to Him, dear friend. Experience His eternal love.

NOTHING ON EARTH OR IN
HEAVEN CAN PART
A LOVE THAT HAS GROWN
TO BE PART OF THE HEART;
AND JUST LIKE THE SUN
AND THE STARS AND THE SEA,
THIS LOVE WILL GO ON
THROUGH ETERNITY.
FOR TRUE LOVE LIVES ON
WHEN EARTHLY THINGS DIE,
FOR IT'S PART OF THE SPIRIT
THAT SOARS TO THE SKY.

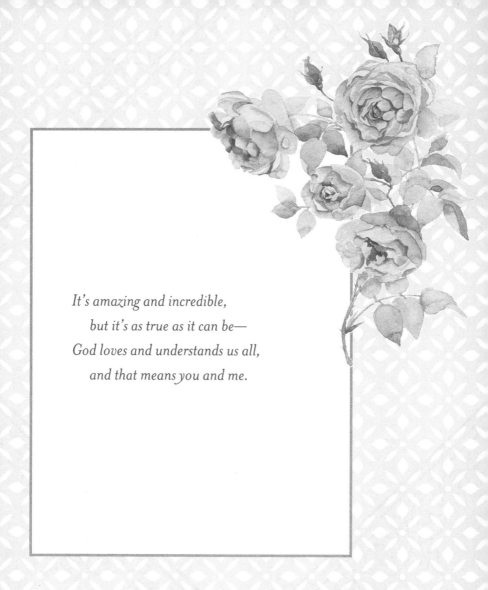

It's amazing and incredible,
but it's as true as it can be—
God loves and understands us all,
and that means you and me.

God's kindness is ever around you,
always ready to freely impart
Strength to your faltering spirit,
cheer to your lonely heart.

So how could I think God
was far, far away
When I feel Him beside me
every hour of the day?
And I've plenty of reasons
to know God's my friend
And this is one friendship
that time cannot end!

Come near to God and
he will come near to you.

JAMES 4:8

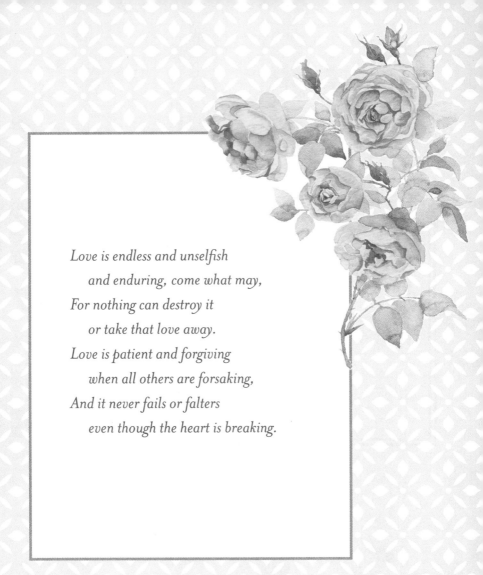

Love is endless and unselfish
   and enduring, come what may,
For nothing can destroy it
   or take that love away.
Love is patient and forgiving
   when all others are forsaking,
And it never fails or falters
   even though the heart is breaking.

Nothing on earth
or in heaven can part
A love that has grown
to be part of the heart.

*[God has] love that is bigger
than race or creed
To cover the world and
fulfill each need.*

God's love endureth forever—
what a wonderful thing to know
When the tides of life run against you
and your spirit is downcast and low.

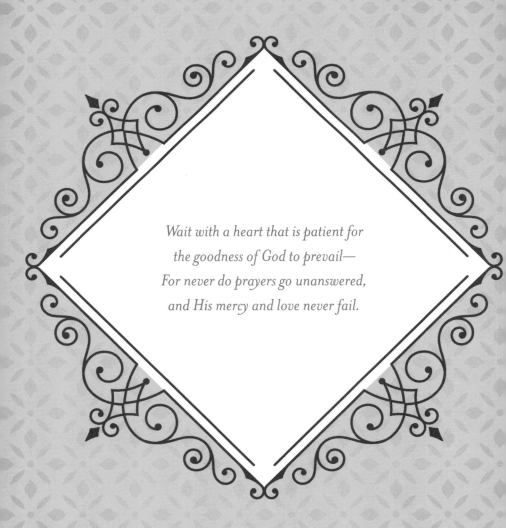

Wait with a heart that is patient for
the goodness of God to prevail—
For never do prayers go unanswered,
and His mercy and love never fail.

*Be still before the L*ORD *and*
wait patiently for him.

PSALM 37:7

Knowing God's love is unfailing,
*   and His mercy unending and great,*
You have but to trust in His promise,
*   "God comes not too soon or too late."*

Just like the sun and
the stars and the sea,
True love will go on
through eternity.

I take thee to be my
partner for life,
To love and live with
as husband and wife;
To have and to hold forever,
sweetheart,
Through sickness and health
until death do us part.

Through long, happy years of
caring and sharing,
Secure in the knowledge that we are preparing
A love that is endless and never can die
But finds its fulfillment with You in the sky.

Let me serve You every day
And feel You near me when I pray.
Oh, hear my prayer, dear God above,
And make me worthy of Your love.

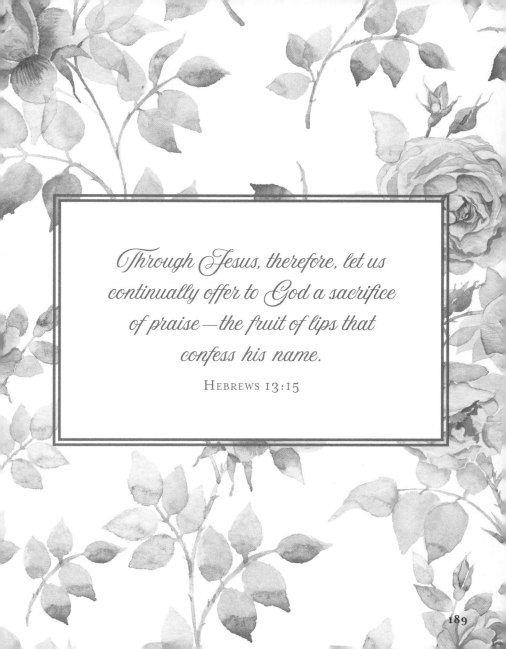

Through Jesus, therefore, let us continually offer to God a sacrifice of praise—the fruit of lips that confess his name.

HEBREWS 13:15

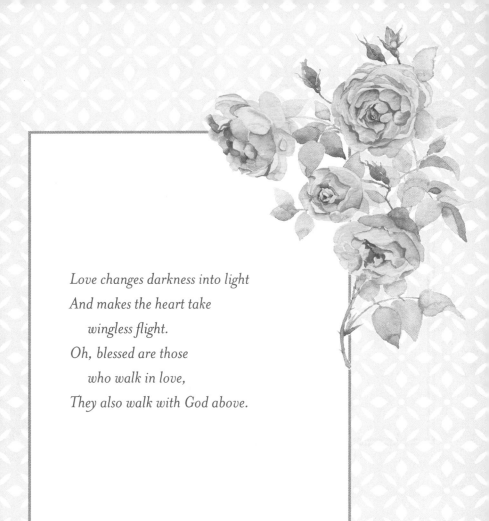

Love changes darkness into light
And makes the heart take
wingless flight.
Oh, blessed are those
who walk in love,
They also walk with God above.

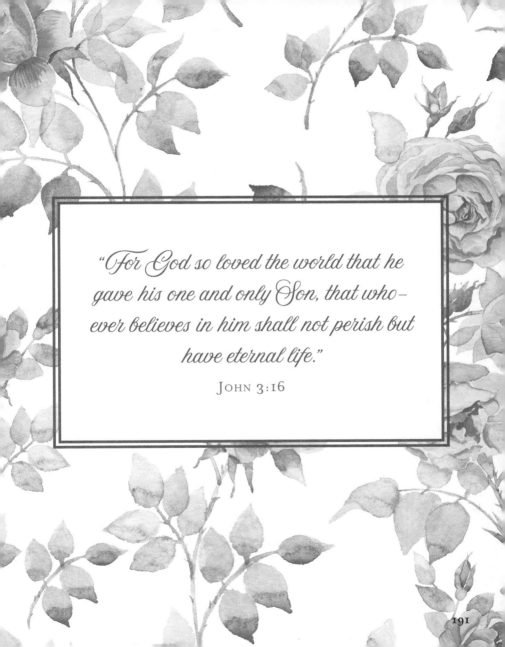

"For God so loved the world that he gave his one and only Son, that who-ever believes in him shall not perish but have eternal life."

JOHN 3:16

America's beloved inspirational poet laureate, **Helen Steiner Rice**, has encouraged millions of people through her beautiful and uplifting verse. Born in Lorain, Ohio, in 1900, Helen was the daughter of a railroad man and an accomplished seamstress and began writing poetry at a young age.

In 1918, Helen began working for a public utilities company and eventually became one of the first female advertising managers and public speakers in the country. In January 1929, she married a wealthy banker named Franklin Rice, who later sank into depression during the Great Depression and eventually committed suicide. Helen later said that her suffering made her sensitive to the pain of others. Her sadness helped her to write some of her most uplifting verses.

Her work for a Cincinnati, Ohio, greeting card company eventually led to her nationwide popularity as a poet when her Christmas card poem "The Priceless Gift of Christmas" was first read on *The Lawrence Welk Show*. Soon Helen had produced several books of her poetry that were a source of inspiration to millions of readers.

Helen died in 1981, leaving a foundation in her name to offer assistance to the needy and the elderly. Now decades after her death, Helen's words still speak powerfully to the hearts of readers about love and comfort, faith and hope, peace and joy.